From Labor to Leadership

A Beginner's Guide to Wealth: Financial Strategies for Everyday People

Brett Pichla

First Edition

NEWMAN SPRINGS PUBLISHING
Meadville, PA

First originally published by Newman Springs Publishing 2025

ISBN 979-8-89617-621-3 (Paperback)
ISBN 979-8-89617-622-0 (Digital)

Printed in the United States of America

To my younger self, who never stopped dreaming of a better future, and to everyone who has ever felt lost navigating the world of finance—this book is for you.

To my wife, whose constant support, love, and encouragement have been my greatest source of strength—your belief in me made this journey possible.

And to the financial authors whose insights illuminated the path forward—your wisdom has been a guiding light. May this book serve as a stepping stone for others seeking financial freedom and a brighter future.

Contents

Preface ix
Chapter 1: Introduction 1
Chapter 2: Shifting-Your-Money Mindset 14
Chapter 3: Wealth Creation Vehicles 30
3.1 Equity-Based Vehicles 31
3.2 Debt-Based Vehicles 37
3.3 Cash and Cash-Equivalent Vehicles 42
3.4 Alternative Investment Vehicles 47
3.5 Retirement Vehicles 51
Chapter 4: Applying Wealth-Building Strategies 58
4.1 Establishing a Baseline 60
4.2 Retirement Investment Options 63
4.3 Beyond Retirement 76

Conclusion..83
Appendix...85
Glossary of Financial Terms..................................91
References 99

Preface

I know what it's like to feel that wealth and financial security are out of reach, reserved for a select few. I started my journey with hard work and grit, never imagining I'd one day be navigating the financial world as a leader. But through experience, I've learned that success isn't about where you start; it's about understanding the system and making it work for you. Now I'm passionate about helping others on that same path, turning financial barriers into stepping stones for a better future.

I have always been an avid learner, primarily inspired by my mother. I grew up in a time when almost every home had a set of encyclopedias—think of it as a paper version of Wikipedia! Whenever I had a question, my mother would encourage me to *look it up*. Although I didn't appreciate this then, it instilled in me the importance of taking control of my destiny and learning how to seek out information.

Since then, I have never stopped researching and learning, and I am now pursuing a doctorate in business administration. At forty-five, I have been very fortunate and, with my wife's encouragement, decided to share what I have learned. This guide is designed to help those who want to establish a secure financial future but may not have the time or interest in financial management. It aims to empower individuals to take control of their finances. Although the material targets those new to investing, it can serve as a springboard and catalyst for those who want to learn more.

This guide compiles insights from books, peer-reviewed articles, and online research conducted by leading figures in business, investing, and wealth creation, alongside my personal experiences by trial and error. My goal is to reach individuals in circumstances like mine, helping those who may not have been born with the financial acumen that often characterizes those who publish financial advice. This book embodies years of research, application, and lessons learned as I advanced in these fields.

I strive to cut through the fluff and provide real-world financial advice on building wealth and leveraging resources to achieve your goals. I do not propose "get rich quick" schemes or "easy money" tactics. That said, I'm not a money manager or financial planner. It's easy to fall into those modes of thinking, especially in today's social media–driven society, where everyone seems to be living the *perfect* life. Unfortunately (well, not for those who capitalize on it), many have become wealthy by leveraging this fact and taking advantage of others.

While there are likely other avenues for wealth creation that are not discussed here, I focus on those that continue to produce results. I only offer life lessons and alternatives I wish had been distilled down for me when I was growing up. I appreciate your interest and wish you all the best in your financial endeavors.

Chapter 1

Introduction

Wealth creation is the process of building financial security and long-term prosperity by growing assets, making smart investments, and leveraging opportunities. It's about generating value through work, entrepreneurship, and strategic decision-making to improve one's financial well-being and future stability beyond just money.

Unfortunately, many individuals lack the financial literacy needed to effectively manage and grow their wealth, which can have long-term consequences for their financial stability. As people live longer, financial literacy in the United States remains surprisingly low. Many students go through their grade-school years without a single finance class, leaving them unprepared to navigate real-world financial decisions. This gap is even more pronounced in socially disadvantaged communities—like the one I grew up in—where underfunded schools struggled with low rankings and limited academic resources.

For many students in these environments, challenges in subjects like mathematics further compounded the issue. With low proficiency rates and little academic support, career recommendations often reflected these struggles rather than students' true potential. I experienced this firsthand as my academic labors shaped the paths presented to me, often steering me toward immediate employment rather than higher education.

Despite my aspirations of attending college after high school, financial reality quickly set in. The local community college offered only a Pell Grant—just $200 a year—barely enough to cover a single textbook. With limited financial support and the pressing need to contribute to my household, immediate employment became the only viable option for me.

Yet the pursuit of a brighter future never faded. Balancing factory work by day and attending community college at night, progress came slowly but steadily. Over time, persistence paid off, earning a bachelor's degree at thirty and a master's at thirty-five—a journey that underscored just how critical financial literacy is in shaping one's future.

This lack of financial knowledge isn't just an individual challenge—it's a systemic issue, particularly in marginalized communities where education gaps are stark. Without foundational financial skills, many students are left unprepared for adulthood, limiting their economic mobility and long-term success.

As an adult, I had the opportunity to volunteer with Junior Achievement, a nonprofit dedicated to inspiring young people (K–12) through financial literacy, career readiness, and entrepreneurship. Through on-site workshops led by organizational and community leaders, Junior Achievement brings financial education directly into classrooms—particularly in underrepresented communities.

However, my time in the classroom revealed a harsh reality. As I walked through school metal detectors and attempted to engage with students, it quickly became apparent that financial literacy was the least of their concerns. For many, the immediate struggle was survival—securing shelter, safety, and food—leaving little room to focus on budgeting or saving.

This experience reinforced the urgent need for a more holistic approach to financial education, one that not only teaches practical money management but also acknowledges and addresses the deeper socioeconomic barriers preventing students from planning their futures. True financial empowerment must go beyond lessons on savings and investing; it must meet students where they are and provide the resources, mentorship, and support they need to break the cycle of poverty.

Unfortunately, these issues accumulate and continue into adulthood, with data showing significant disparities in financial education. In 2023, only *40.5 percent of high schoolers* were *guaranteed to take a personal finance course.*[1] Additionally, a U.S. Federal Reserve report on the economic well-being of U.S. households (2022–May 2023) revealed that just 60 percent of adults could correctly answer financial literacy questions, meaning 40% lacked essential financial knowledge (see Table 1).

Table 1. Share of financial literacy questions answered correctly (by retirement savings and comfort investing).[2]

Presence of retirement savings and level of investing comfort	Percent
Has self-directed retirement savings	68
• Mostly or very comfortable investing	77
• Not or slightly comfortable investing	63
No self-directed retirement savings	37
Retired	65
Overall	**60**

Note: Among all adults.

And so, the cycle continues for individuals who are uncertain about how to navigate their financial futures. As a result, many young adults, like me, lack a clear understanding of investing. Unfortunately, most are not introduced to investment concepts until they are older, often through their employers. By this time, they face multiple obstacles, such as deciding what to invest in and the valuable time lost during their formative years for investment and growth. This leaves them scrambling to catch up in order to secure some form of retirement and makes them highly susceptible to a financial system that is more than happy to exploit their lack of understanding.

The impact of financial literacy extends beyond individuals, affecting entire families. Parents who lack confidence in their own financial knowledge struggle to guide their children, perpetuating a cycle of uncertainty. In fact, *over 75 percent of parents report not being completely confident in their ability to teach their children about investing.*[3] With *57 percent of Americans living paycheck to paycheck*, financial insecurity remains a persistent issue, limiting opportunities for wealth-building and long-term stability.[4]

This issue is particularly evident in retirement preparedness. As represented in Figure 1, *while nearly three-fourths of non-retired adults had at least some retirement savings, 28 percent had none.*[5] A review of Table 2 reveals that the situation is even more pronounced among younger adults, *who were both less likely to have retirement savings and to view their savings as on track.*[6] Specifically, 57 percent of those aged 18–29 and 72 percent aged 30–44 had some retirement savings, meaning approximately 43 percent and 28 percent in those age groups had none.

Figure 1. Forms of retirement savings among non-retirees.[7]

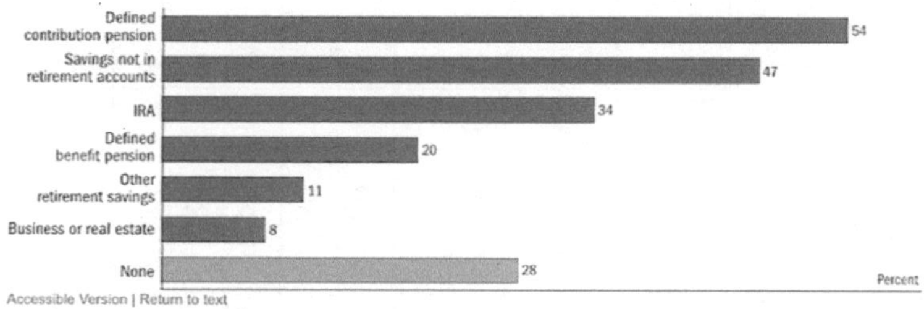

Note: Among non-retirees. Respondents could select multiple answers.

Additionally illustrated in Table 2, *compared with all non-retires, Black and Hispanic non-retirees were less likely to have retirement savings and to view their retirement savings as on track.*[8]

Table 2. Have retirement savings and view retirement savings plan as on track (by age, race/ethnicity, and disability status).[9]

Characteristic	**Any retirement savings (%)**	**Retirement savings on track (%)**
Age		
18–29	57	24
30–44	72	32
45–59	81	34
60+	88	41
Race/ethnicity		
White	80	37
Black	60	22
Hispanic	56	20
Asian	84	38
Disability status		
No disability	76	34
Disability	47	13
Overall	72	31

Note: Among non-retirees.

These figures are concerning yet emphasize the importance and need for this book. Although different individuals have varying perceptions of financial security, and these views can evolve, the principles of wealth creation are consistent regardless of demographics. The key differences lie in the amount invested, the types and sizes of investments, and the frequency of those investments.

I don't want to sugarcoat things—life can sometimes be challenging. We often try to avoid pain, but embracing it can lead to greater happiness. You might be wondering how this relates to financial security. It took me years to truly understand this lesson, and I frequently need to remind myself to refocus. At its core, I'm talking about delayed gratification, which is the foundation of wealth creation—acting today to prepare for the future. Contrary to what you may have heard, it doesn't involve dedicating one's life to pursuing wealth. However, no one is stopping you if you wish to do so. What it does require is consistent action.

Today, avoiding the effort needed to take control of your future is easier than ever. We all fall into this trap, often distracted by TV, social media, the internet, and email, among other things, all vying for our attention. However, as Dave Ramsey once said, *You must gain control over your money, or the lack of it will forever control you.*[10] This doesn't mean you need to become a wealth manager, but you should spend some time and effort learning the basics to make your money work for you instead of you working for it.

However, by purchasing this book, you have already taken the first step toward that goal, and this short book aims to distill that knowledge. Everyone desires what others have. The truth is that those who build wealth do so by earning more money than they spend. Wealth generation requires hard work, and those who accumulate wealth and retain it—*retain* being the key term—have worked diligently and learned how to make their money work for them.

While there are family dynasties that have stood the test of time, it's important to remember that their wealth often started with initial hard work. However, *70 percent of wealthy families lose their wealth by the next generation, with 90 percent losing it in the generation after that.*[11] This often occurs because those later generations did not participate in the wealth-building process and, as a result, never learned how to sustain it. This phenomenon explains why we often hear stories of individuals who acquire wealth quickly—such as lottery winners or celebrities—only to lose it just as rapidly.

Understanding these principles is crucial for achieving a secure financial future, even though it may seem simple and is often not explained in detail. Those who successfully keep their wealth leverage their additional finances to work for them. If you are beginning your career or are economically stretched, you may wonder, "What are *extra* finances?" We will cover that in more detail later in the book, but keep this idea in mind for now.

In the following chapters, we will discuss shifting your money mindset, wealth creation vehicles, and developing strategies—each building upon the other. The book is written from the perspective of an individual following a typical career trajectory within the United States. By the end, you will have a different perception toward wealth creation and understand the various options available to create wealth and potential roadmaps for achieving it. If I can do it, you can too, so let's get started!

Chapter Summary and Action Steps

Congratulations on completing Chapter 1! To help you navigate the book more effectively, each chapter will conclude with a summary and action steps. These action steps are linked to the Activity Checklist found in the Appendix. You can complete each step as you progress or print the Checklist in advance.

This chapter highlighted the pressing issue of financial illiteracy in the United States, particularly in underserved communities where underfunded schools and limited academic resources leave students unprepared to navigate real-world financial decisions. Many young adults, like me, are introduced to investing and financial planning too late—often through their employers—resulting in lost opportunities for early financial security.

The cycle continues into adulthood, where financial uncertainty affects individuals and entire families, with parents struggling to pass on financial knowledge to their children. Alarming statistics highlight that 40 percent of adults lack essential financial knowledge, 57 percent of Americans live paycheck to paycheck, and nearly 28 percent of non-retired adults have no retirement savings.

Despite these challenges, financial success is possible with the right mindset and consistent action. Wealth creation is not about chasing money relentlessly but about making informed financial decisions, practicing delayed gratification, and leveraging resources effectively. This book serves as a guide to help readers shift their financial mindset, explore wealth-building strategies, and develop practical approaches to securing their financial future.

1. *Start tracking your spending:* Create a spreadsheet with four columns—date, debit, credit, and category. In the debit column, list all money spent, including expenses from credit cards and bank statements. In the credit column, record any money earned. For each transaction, provide a brief description in the category column, such as *dining out*, *vehicle expense*, and so on, but keep them consistent (for example, under vehicle expenses, include gas, repairs, and accessories such as air fresheners).
   - Be sure to include the date of each transaction. Work backward for three months, then total up the debit and credit columns. Is there more money in the debit than credit? Which categories are you spending the most? Are there areas where you can save?
   - Note: While it may be tempting to use automated processes to track your spending, it's essential to do this manually, especially at the beginning. This will help you gain a clearer understanding of where your money is going (even if you think you do).

Chapter 2

Shifting-Your-Money Mindset

Growing up in a low- to middle-class household, my understanding of investing was limited to keeping money in a savings account. Conversations about retirement or wealth creation were almost nonexistent. The people we surrounded ourselves with shared the same mindset: work hard, keep your head down, and hope to pay off your mortgage by the time you are old enough to collect Social Security and, if you are fortunate, receive a pension.

Transitioning from a laborer to a leader requires a significant shift in mindset, which is why this topic is addressed early in the book. Each individual views the world through a unique lens, which can be understood as a personal bias. The *Cambridge Dictionary* defines bias as *the fact of preferring a particular subject or thing.*[12] This perspective is influenced by various factors, including upbringing, relationships with friends and family, education, personal experiences, and cultural backgrounds. Therefore, changing your mindset often necessitates altering one or more of these factors.

My mindset was changed at the age of twenty and a half, the minimum age for enrollment at the time—when my second employer provided me with paperwork to enroll in the company's retirement account. I was working at a manufacturing company, putting in as many hours as possible to pay off bad debt that I had accumulated from moving out on my own at eighteen and saving desperately for my first house (which I purchased at twenty-one). They encouraged me to enroll in the retirement plan and explained that the company would *match* contributions up to 3 percent of my salary. Essentially, if I contributed at least 3 percent, they would match it, dollar for dollar.

My initial reaction was, "Who doesn't like free money?" But so many questions circled through my brain: Where does the money go? When can I get it back? At the time, retirement wasn't even on my radar, and I had no understanding of what a retirement account was or why contributing to it was necessary—beyond the obvious appeal of the company match.

Being the researcher I was, I immediately went to the library and checked out a book on retirement investing. I was fascinated by compound interest—the idea of making money while you slept. My curiosity grew, and I started consuming as many books as possible by some of the most influential finance experts at the time. The internet was not yet a reliable source of information, so books were a primary resource.

Although I unfortunately suffered a divorce at twenty-five, I had accumulated over $30,000 in my retirement account. My spouse's account, which I helped establish, held nearly the same amount. That was a significant sum back then, especially considering I was earning $12 per hour.

By that point, I had learned enough about investing to hate the idea of borrowing against my retirement account to settle the divorce. While I understood that I'd repay the loan over the agreed-upon terms, the thought of lost investment gains due to money being temporarily out of the market was painful. However, having the funds available made the divorce process far easier to navigate. I also learned a valuable lesson—as Warren Buffett wisely stated, that *if you don't make money while you sleep, you will work until you die.*[13]

This experience reinforced just how critical it is to start saving and investing early. Yet despite the clear advantages of early investing, a staggering *43.5 percent of full-time working Americans do not participate* in employer-sponsored plans.[14] This lack of participation can have significant long-term consequences, as delaying retirement contributions even by a decade can drastically reduce the amount one accumulates over time. The power of compound interest means that the earlier one begins, the more money works for them.

For instance, **a *twenty-five-year-old*** *who saves $500 a month until age 65, assuming a 7 percent return, would accumulate nearly* ***$1.2 million.***[15] *In contrast, a* ***thirty-five-year-old*** who starts saving the same amount under the same conditions would only *have approximately $567,000 by age sixty-five*—less than half of what the earlier saver would amass. [16] This difference highlights why financial literacy and early retirement planning are essential.

The impact of investment is even more pronounced when higher returns are considered. If you look at Figure 2, imagine you start with just *$1,000 and add $100 a month to your savings for thirty-five years.*[17] Without investing, you would *have $43,000 (gold graph line)*. However, if you invested the exact amount and *earned a 10 percent* average annual return, your balance would grow to over *$370,000 (purple graph line).*[18] A staggering difference of over *$300,000* just by investing vs. saving.

Yet millions of Americans miss out on these opportunities either due to lack of knowledge, financial constraints, or the misconception that they can *catch up* later.

Figure 2. How compound interest affects your money.[19]

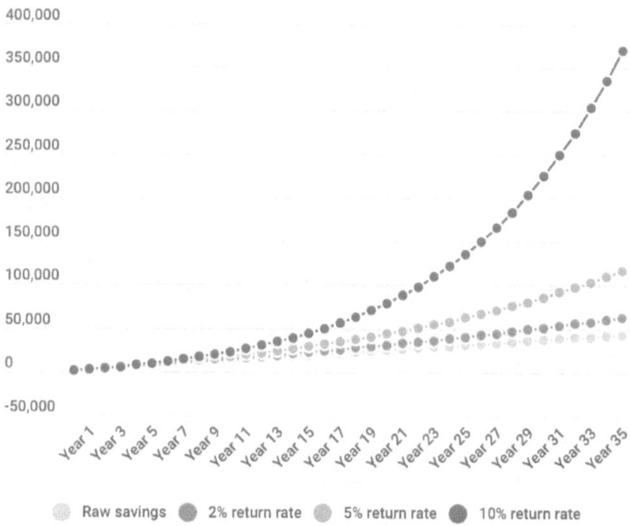

Ultimately, the numbers make a compelling case for prioritizing retirement savings as early as possible. While financial hardships and competing priorities can make it challenging to contribute consistently, even small contributions can make a significant impact over time. Taking advantage of employer-sponsored plans, contributing enough to receive an employer match, and investing wisely can set the foundation for long-term financial security.

A 2023 Gallup poll identified three key factors influencing stock ownership in the U.S.: *household income, education, and age.*[20] The data revealed stark disparities in participation based on these factors. Specifically, ***84 percent of adults*** *in households earning* ***$100,000*** *or more* ***own stocks***, compared to only ***29 percent*** *of those in households earning* ***less than $40,000.***[21] Similarly, education plays a significant role—***82 percent of postgraduates own stocks***, while only ***41 percent*** *of individuals with a* ***high school education*** *or less do.*[22] Age is another determining factor, with ***41 percent*** *of* adults ***aged eighteen to twenty-eight*** investing in *stocks* versus ***63 percent*** *of those* ***aged sixty-five and older.***[23]

These statistics reinforce a broader reality: financial participation is often dictated by one's stage in life and the available resources. Like my own experience, younger individuals and those with lower income or educational attainment are less likely to invest, not necessarily due to a lack of interest, but because their financial priorities are focused elsewhere. This hesitancy or inability to invest can have long-term consequences, as delayed market participation significantly reduces the potential for wealth accumulation through compounding returns.

This trend aligns with Maslow's Hierarchy of Needs (Figure 3), which explains human motivation in a tiered structure, with *physiological (survival) needs* forming the foundation *and self-actualization* (the pursuit of personal growth and fulfillment) *at the top.*[24] For individuals who are just starting their careers or struggling to make ends meet, financial priorities are naturally centered on immediate necessities—housing, food, healthcare, and other essentials—rather than long-term investments. Retirement planning and wealth-building strategies often take a backseat when financial security is uncertain.

Figure 3. Maslow's Hierarchy of Needs.[25]

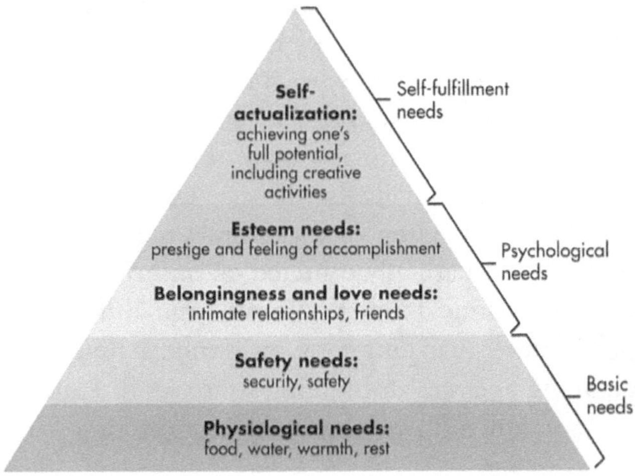

Further supporting this idea, Lee and Hanna's study, *Savings Goals and Saving Behavior From a Perspective of Maslow's Hierarchy of Needs*, found that only *2 percent of respondents identified self-actualization as a financial goal,* reinforcing Maslow's theory that relatively few people reach the higher levels of the hierarchy with *strong aspirations* for long-term wealth.[26] The challenge is finding ways to bridge this gap—ensuring that financial literacy, accessible investment opportunities, and policy interventions help individuals move beyond survival-based financial decisions and toward long-term wealth-building strategies.

Understanding these financial disparities and psychological factors made me reflect on my own journey. Like many others, I once faced the challenge of balancing immediate financial obligations with long-term investment goals. However, a pivotal moment came when my employer handed me my retirement paperwork—a tangible reminder that financial security in the future depended on the decisions I made today.

I chose to act—not just by enrolling in retirement plans but by committing to continuous learning and personal growth. Similarly, reading this book is a step toward enhancing your understanding and inspiring you to seek additional knowledge, whether by exploring related materials or applying these concepts to your daily life. I knew I didn't want to work forever, and more importantly, I wanted to build a life I could truly enjoy.

I began to measure my financial position more carefully. I stopped worrying about or comparing myself to others; instead, I focused on increasing my income, such as obtaining a degree—one of the first in my family—investing wisely, and spending thoughtfully. Every purchase became a matter of necessity. This doesn't mean you stop living; instead, it encourages you to evaluate and reflect on what living truly means to you. For instance, are you working for a company that offers education assistance?

Many employers offer educational assistance programs. While I initially paid some tuition out of pocket, I was fortunate that my first employer covered my bachelor's degree, and my second funded my master's. If you're considering furthering your education—whether you're just starting your career or already established—don't hesitate to ask your employer if they provide tuition assistance.

If they do, the approval process typically begins with your manager and then moves to human resources. It's not uncommon for employers to cover some or even all the costs of higher education, often with a contractual obligation requiring you to stay with the company for a set period (usually two to three years) after completing your degree. If you or the company choose to part ways before fulfilling that commitment, you may be required to repay some of the funding. However, repayment is usually not needed in layoffs or early retirement.

When I pursued my master's degree, I knew I'd stay with my company for at least five years, so I started my program soon after joining. If continuing your education is a goal, leveraging employer-sponsored assistance can be a valuable way to achieve it without the entire financial burden. Additionally, many employers offer a pay raise upon earning a degree, which can contribute to your financial goals. Be sure to inquire with your manager or human resources department about available options.

Beyond education, financial growth also requires a shift in mindset. Many people, especially those in labor-intensive roles, view money in a linear way—working for a paycheck, spending it, and repeating the cycle. However, true financial empowerment comes from learning how to make money work for you. This transition from laborer to leadership can be difficult, particularly at the beginning. It's even more challenging when financial systems seem designed to benefit those who already have leverage.

Consider, for example, the impact of high-interest debt. *The average credit card interest rate on accounts with balances* is at *23.37 percent.*[27] *According to TransUnion*, the average credit card balance per consumer was *$6,380 in 2024.*[28] If only the minimum payment due was made each month, it would take approximately four years and three months to pay off the balance. In this scenario, the total interest paid would be approximately $3,687, meaning the individual would have paid nearly $10,000 in total!

In contrast, if the same $6,380 were instead invested and grew at an average net rate of 7%—the historical US market return—after the same four-year period, it would grow to approximately $8,362, assuming no other contributions were made. This example highlights the fundamental truth: understanding interest is critical. Interest represents the cost of borrowing money or the payment received for lending money. Everyone needs cash to purchase goods and services, but cash typically incurs a charge—expressed as an annual percentage rate (APY)—when borrowed. The key is to minimize the interest paid to others while maximizing the interest earned from investments. You work hard for your money, so you want it to work just as hard for you.

To achieve this, focus on reducing your debt while increasing investments. Various strategies are beyond the scope of this guide, and individual circumstances will differ. However, the core mindset remains the same: strive to earn more than you spend, reduce your debt, and invest wisely. This is a long-term endeavor; the sooner you begin, the greater the benefits you'll reap. The most important step is simply starting—even if your initial progress seems small. As Warren Buffett cautioned, *People who hold cash equivalents feel comfortable; they shouldn't. They have opted for a terrible long-term asset that pays virtually nothing and is certain to depreciate in value.*[29]

We will continue to expand on these concepts throughout the book, but for now, take a moment to assess your current situation. Are you beginning to see areas where you can make changes? How has your perspective started to shift? Consider the mindset of those around you—your family, friends, or coworkers. Are their aspirations shaping yours, or do you have your own unique financial goals? Are you actively steering your financial future, or is it steering you? Do you have a plan for where you want to be financially this year, next year, or even at retirement?

If you don't have all the answers yet, don't worry. If you did, you wouldn't be reading this book. What matters is that you're starting to think about these questions. My hope is that the insights in this book will serve as a roadmap and encourage you to keep progressing. Try not to become overwhelmed. Life is a series of moments, and this is just one of them. Let's continue our journey together!

Chapter Summary and Action Steps

This chapter explored the transformation from a laborer's financial mindset to that of a leader by emphasizing the importance of investing, financial literacy, and strategic planning. My personal journey is shared of growing up in a low- to middle-class household with limited exposure to wealth-building strategies. A pivotal moment occurred at age twenty-plus when my employer introduced a retirement plan, sparking a deep interest in investing in financial growth.

The chapter highlighted the power of compound interest, the disparities in stock ownership across income and education levels, and the influence of Maslow's hierarchy of needs on financial priorities. I stress the value of employee-sponsored education benefits, the impact of interest rates on debt, and the necessity of shifting from earning money linearly to making it work for you.

Lastly, I encourage readers to evaluate their financial mindset, with the chapter setting the stage for deeper financial exploration throughout the book.

2. *Access your money mindset:* Create a three-to-five-year plan. Be realistic, but the goals you create

should challenge you. Start by considering the following:

- Personal development: What skills, certifications, or degrees do you want to acquire? Are there specific areas you want to focus on, such as health, relationships, or personal growth?
- Career: Where do you want to be in your career? Are you looking for a promotion, a career change, or a new skill set?
- Finances: Does your employer offer education assistance? Are there any spending habits identified in step one that need to change? Begin identifying your debt (we will discuss more in Chapter 4).
- *Break down long-term plans into actionable goals*: What do you need to do this year, this month, and today to achieve these goals?

Chapter 3

Wealth Creation Vehicles

In this chapter, we will review the various vehicles for wealth creation. While this list is by no means exhaustive, it highlights some common approaches with a proven history of generating wealth. These include:

1. *Equity-based vehicles*: This category encompasses stocks, exchange-traded funds (ETFs), and mutual funds.
2. *Debt-based vehicles*: These include bonds.
3. *Cash and cash-equivalent vehicles*: Examples are savings accounts, certificates of deposit

(CDs), money market accounts, and high-yield savings accounts.

4. *Alternative investment vehicles*: Real estate falls into this category.
5. *Retirement-specific vehicles*: This includes 401(k) and 403(b) plans, individual retirement accounts (IRAs), Roth IRAs, and pension plans.

Every one of these vehicles can help individuals build wealth over time. As with any financial decision, it is always advised to consult with a tax professional. They are in the best position to provide guidance, especially since financial regulations are constantly changing.

3.1 Equity-Based Vehicles

When it comes to building wealth over time, equity-based vehicles are among the most powerful tools. At their core, these investments—stocks, exchange-traded funds (ETFs), and mutual funds—allow individuals to participate in the financial success of companies. While the world of investing may seem complex or intimidating at first, understanding the fundamentals can make it far more approachable.

In simple terms, businesses need money to grow, whether for expansion, research, or other initiatives. One way they raise this capital is by selling ownership shares—known as stock—to investors in exchange for cash. These stocks are then bought and sold on financial marketplaces called stock exchanges, such as the New York Stock Exchange (NYSE) or Nasdaq.

Stock exchanges serve as a trusted marketplace where investors can trade shares in an organized and regulated environment. While stock trading today happens almost instantly through online platforms, the concept of exchanges dates back centuries. The first known exchange was established in *1531*, and in the U.S., the Philadelphia Stock Exchange was founded in *1790,* followed by the New York Stock Exchange in *1792.*[30,31] Early traders conducted transactions in person using slips of paper, but today, these trades are executed electronically, making investing more accessible than ever.

How brokerage firms help you invest

For an individual investor, buying and selling stocks directly from an exchange isn't always possible. This is where brokerage firms come in. Brokerages—such as fidelity investments, T. Rowe Price, or Charles Schwab—act as intermediaries, facilitating trades on behalf of investors. They employ brokers (sometimes called stockbrokers or securities brokers) who execute transactions in exchange for a fee or commission.

There are two primary types of brokerages:

- *Full-service brokerages*: These firms provide personalized investment advice, research, and portfolio management, often catering to investors who prefer expert guidance.
- *Discount brokerages*: These platforms, such as Robinhood or E*Trade, allow investors to trade stocks with minimal fees and without requiring a professional advisor.

While most full-service brokerages now provide options for investing with or without assistance, the right type of brokerage for you depends on your investment strategy, experience level, and comfort with managing your own portfolio. We'll explore investment strategies in greater detail in the next chapter.

Understanding risk and return

One of the most important things to remember about equity-based investments is that their value depends on the performance of the companies they represent. This makes them inherently riskier than other types of investments, as stock prices can rise and fall due to factors like market conditions, company earnings, and economic trends. However, despite these fluctuations, history has shown that stocks tend to grow in value over the long term.

In fact, the U.S. stock market has historically delivered an average *real return* (adjusted for inflation) of around *7.0 percent* per year.[32] While no investment is completely *safe*—as demonstrated by financial crises like the Great Depression of 1929 and the Great Recession of 2007—avoiding investing altogether can be even riskier. Recall Buffett's quote from Chapter 2:

> *If you don't make money while you sleep, you will work until you die.*[33]

The power of pooled investments: ETFs and mutual funds

For many investors, particularly beginners, buying individual stocks can feel overwhelming. Instead of picking and managing the stocks individually, pooled investments like *mutual funds* and *exchange-traded funds* (ETFs) offer a way to invest in a diversified portfolio of assets.

Both ETFs and mutual funds function similarly to stocks in that they can be bought and sold on the market. However, they hold multiple securities—such as stocks, bonds, or other assets—bundled together into a single investment. This diversification helps reduce risk compared to investing in a single company.

- *Mutual funds*: Typically managed by professional fund managers, mutual funds are designed to achieve a specific investment goal, such as growth, income, or stability. Some funds are actively managed, meaning fund managers decide which assets to buy or sell based on market conditions. Others are passively managed, meaning they track a market index like the S&P 500.
- *ETFs*: These funds operate similarly to mutual funds but trade on stock exchanges like individual stocks. ETFs often have lower fees than mutual funds and can be a cost-effective way for investors to gain exposure to different market sectors.

What are market indices and why do they matter?

A market index is a collection of stocks or other financial assets that represent a particular market segment's performance. Some of the most well-known indices include:

- *The S&P 500*: Tracks five hundred of the largest U.S. companies and serves as a key benchmark for the overall market.
- *The Dow Jones Industrial Average* (the Dow): Comprises thirty major U.S. companies and is one of the oldest stock market indices.

Although investors cannot buy shares of an index itself, they can invest in index-linked funds, which are designed to mimic the performance of a specific index. These funds, such as index mutual funds and index ETFs, offer a passive investment approach that has grown in popularity since the launch of the *first index fund in 1976*.[34]

Final thoughts: building your investment knowledge

Equity-based investments, while carrying some risk, have historically been one of the best ways to build long-term wealth. Whether you choose individual stocks, ETFs, or mutual funds, understanding how these vehicles work can help you make informed financial decisions. As we continue exploring investment strategies in the next chapter, consider how these options align with your personal goals and risk tolerance.

If you're new to investing, don't be discouraged by the complexity—it's a learning process, and you're already taking an important step by educating yourself. The key takeaway? Investing isn't just for financial professionals or the wealthy—it's for anyone looking to build a more secure future.

3.2 Debt-Based Vehicles

When most people think about investing, they often picture the stock market. However, another major category of investments—debt-based vehicles, also known as fixed-income securities—play a crucial role in both personal and institutional portfolios. These investments focus on lending money rather than owning a stake in a company.

At its core, a debt-based investment is when an investor lends money to an entity, typically a government or corporation, in exchange for regular interest payments and the eventual return of the original amount (known as the principal) at a specified future date. The most common type of debt-based investment is a bond.

Bonds are often seen as a more stable alternative to stocks because they provide predictable returns. While they may not provide the same potential for rapid growth as equities, they can be a valuable tool for balancing risk, generating income, and preserving capital in an investment portfolio.

How bonds work

A bond is a loan that an investor gives to an organization. In return, the issuing entity agrees to:

- Pay the investor interest payments, called coupons, at a set rate.
- Repay the face value of the bond when it reaches its maturity date.

Here is a simple example. Imagine a company needs to raise $500,000 for a new facility. Instead of taking out a traditional bank loan, it decides to issue 500 bonds at $1,000 each. If these bonds have a ten-year term and a 6 percent annual coupon, each bondholder will receive $60 per year in interest ($1,000 × 6%). At the end of the ten-year period, the company repays the full $1,000 face value of each bond, and the investor will have made $600 ($60 per year in interest).

Because the bondholder knows precisely how much they will earn each year and when they will be repaid, bonds are considered more predictable than stocks.

Comparing bonds and stocks: what's the difference?

Unlike stocks, which represent ownership in a company and fluctuate based on business performance, bonds are structured agreements with predefined repayment terms. However, that does not mean bonds are risk-free. The level of risk depends on several factors:

- *Bond duration*: Shorter-term (e.g., five years) generally have less risk than longer-term bonds (e.g., thirty years), as they are less exposed to market changes and economic shifts.
- *Credit rating*: Bonds are rated based on the issuer's ability to repay its debt. Credit rating agencies like Moody's, S&P, and Fitch assign scores to bonds, ranging from high-quality (low-risk) to lower-quality (high-risk or *junk* bonds).

Higher-risk bonds typically offer higher interest rates to compensate investors for the increased uncertainty of repayment. While both stocks and bonds carry the risk of an issuer defaulting, bonds provide a structured repayment schedule that makes them a more predictable income source when held to maturity.

What happens if a bond issuer defaults?

Although bonds are generally safer than stocks, there is still default risk—the possibility that the issuer will be unable to meet its financial obligations. In cases of bankruptcy, repayment follows a strict hierarchy, as outlined in Figure 4.

- *Senior debt holders* (typically banks and institutional lenders) are the first to be repaid.
- *Bondholders* come next—often receiving at least partial repayment from the company's remaining assets.
- *Stockholders* are last in line and usually receive nothing if the company fails.

This priority system explains why bonds are viewed as lower risk than stocks: even in the worst-case scenario, bondholders stand a better chance of recovering some of their investment.

Figure 4. Hierarchy of repayment.[35]

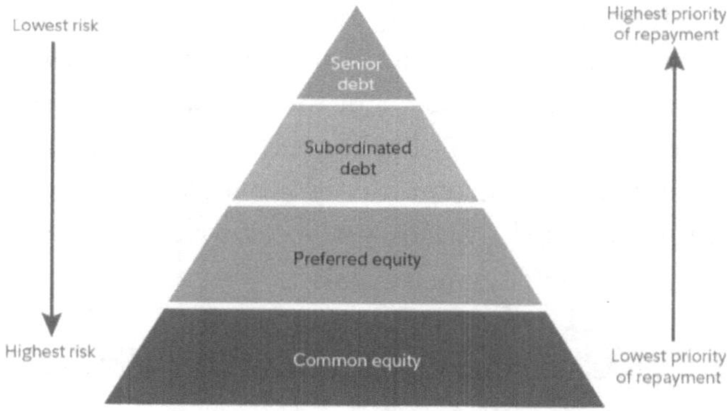

Why Consider Bonds?

For many investors, bonds serve as a stabilizing force in their portfolio. Here's why they can be a smart addition to an investment strategy:

- *Reliable income*: Bonds provide consistent interest payments, making them ideal for retirees or those looking for steady returns.
- *Lower risk than stocks*: While not risk-free, bonds are generally less volatile than the stock market.
- *Portfolio diversification*: Bonds help balance out the ups and downs of stocks, reducing overall investment risk.

While we've discussed passive bond principles (buying bonds to hold until maturity), those who are interested in actively buying and selling bonds need to consider additional factors—many of which extend beyond the scope of this book. Regardless of whether you're planning for retirement, building a passive income stream, or simply looking to reduce investment risk, bonds can be a valuable tool in achieving your financial goals.

3.3 Cash and Cash-Equivalent Vehicles

Cash and cash-equivalent investment vehicles—such as savings accounts, certificates of deposit, money market accounts, and high-yield savings accounts—play a crucial role in a well-rounded financial strategy. These options offer stability, liquidity, and security, making them an excellent place to store emergency funds or short-term savings.

While these vehicles tend to have lower returns than stocks or bonds, they are also among the safest investments available. Their low risk typically comes with benefits such as quick access to funds, lower investment requirements, and FDIC insurance (which covers up to $250,000 per depositor at FDIC-insured banks). Although cash investments alone may not build significant wealth over time, they're an essential foundation for financial security.

The role of interest rates: how the federal reserve impacts cash investments

Interest rates for cash-equivalent vehicles are closely tied to the Federal Reserve—the central banking system in the U.S. The Fed has several responsibilities, but the most important takeaway for investors is that it raises and lowers interest rates to control inflation:

- *When inflation rises*, the Fed *increases* interest rates to slow down borrowing and spending.
- *When the economy slows*, the Fed *lowers* interest rates to encourage borrowing and stimulate growth.

This means that when investment rates are high, savings accounts, CDs, and money market accounts offer better returns—making them more attractive investment options. However, when rates are low, these vehicles may not keep pace with inflation, reducing their real value over time.

Savings accounts: a safe and simple starting point

For many, a savings account is their first introduction to investing. These accounts are:

- *Easy to open*: Often requiring low or no minimum deposit.
- *Highly liquid*: Funds can be accessed at any time, making them ideal for emergency savings.
- *Protected*: FDIC insured up to $250,000 per depositor.

Savings accounts are best used for short-term financial goals, emergency funds, or as a backup for checking accounts. Many banks offer automatic transfers to encourage savings, and some impose withdrawal limits to help maintain balances.

However, the trade-off for this convenience and security is low interest rates—typically ranging from 0.01 percent to 0.35 percent APY.

Certificates of deposit (CDs)

Certificates of deposit (CDs) are a type of savings account where you agree to leave your money untouched for a set period, ranging from a few months to several years. In exchange, banks offer a fixed interest rate that is often higher than regular savings accounts.

- *Predictable returns*: Your interest is locked in for the entire CD term.
- *Best for short-term goals*: Ideal for saving for a down payment, vacation, or large purchase.

Typically, higher rates than savings accounts: Rates can exceed 4 percent APY in high-interest environments.

However, CDs are less flexible than other cash investments. Withdrawing funds early can result in penalties, so they are best for those who don't need immediate access to their money.

Money market accounts vs. high-yield savings accounts

Both money market accounts (MMAs) and high-yield savings accounts (HYSAs) offer higher interest rates than traditional savings accounts. They are a great option for earning more on cash savings while still keeping funds relatively accessible.

Money market accounts (MMAs)

- Often include check-writing capabilities and debit card access.

- May require higher minimum balances to avoid fees.
- Typically, pay 4.5 percent to 5 percent APY in a high-rate environment.

High-yield savings accounts (HYSAs)

- Usually offer higher rates than traditional savings accounts.
- Funds are accessible via online transfers but may take longer to withdraw.
- Currently pay around 4 percent APY on average.

If you want easy access to savings with the ability to write checks, a money market account may be a better choice. If maximizing interest is your goal and you don't need frequent withdrawals, a high-yield savings account might be ideal.

Final thoughts: the role of cash investments in your portfolio

While cash and cash-equivalent investments won't make you rich, they serve an important purpose in financial planning. These vehicles:

- *Provide stability*: Unlike stocks and bonds, they carry little to no market risk.

- *Ensure liquidity*: Funds are easily accessible for emergencies or planned expenses.
- *Offer FDIC protection*: Giving peace of mind against bank failures.

Although long-term investing in stocks and bonds is essential for wealth building, having a solid cash reserve is just as important. Whether it's for an emergency fund, a short-term goal, or simply peace of mind, cash investments play a vital role in a well-rounded financial strategy.

3.4 Alternative Investment Vehicles

When it comes to alternative investments, many people often think of cryptocurrency, commodities, or even private equity. While these are important asset classes, this section will focus on one of the most familiar and reliable options: real estate.

For many people, real estate represents more than just a place to live—it's also an opportunity to build wealth. The most common way to invest in real estate is by purchasing a home. For most individuals, owning a home becomes the largest part of their net worth. The financial incentive lies in building equity, which is the difference between the market value of your home and the amount you still owe on your mortgage.

As home prices rise over time and you make mortgage payments, the equity in your property increases, which you can leverage if needed. For example, if your home appreciates in value and you've paid down a portion of your mortgage, the difference becomes an asset that could be used for future investments or loans.

However, real estate isn't without its challenges. Upfront costs—such as a 20 percent down payment to avoid mortgage insurance—can be a significant barrier for many. Additionally, homeowners must also account for unexpected expenses, such as repairs or maintenance, and the possibility that the value of the property may not appreciate or could even decline.

Despite these challenges, real estate historically tends to increase in value. For instance, the median sales price of homes in the U.S. has risen dramatically—from *$19,300 in 1963 to $584,613 in 2023.*[36] However, whether or not to buy a home is a decision with many considerations, which we'll explore in greater detail in the next chapter.

Other real estate investment options

While buying a home is the most traditional form of real estate investment, there are other ways to invest in property without necessarily buying your primary residence. Let's look at some of these options:

Real Estate Investment Trusts (REITs)

One alternative is Real Estate Investment Trusts (REITs). These are companies that own, operate, or finance real estate assets, such as apartment buildings, shopping centers, office spaces, and even data centers. Many REITs are traded on major stock exchanges, making them easy to invest in, like buying stocks.

Investing in REITs allows you to gain exposure to real estate without the need to buy physical property yourself. You can purchase shares of REITs individually or through mutual funds or exchange-traded funds (ETFs). This approach offers a way to diversify your portfolio while reducing some of the risk involved in directly owning property.

However, like stocks, REITs carry risks, such as market fluctuations and the performance of the properties owned by the trust. The value of your investment in a REIT will largely depend on the company's management decisions and the real estate market as a whole.

Owning property for investment purposes

Another option for real estate investors is buying property strictly for investment purposes. This could include purchasing land, residential properties, or commercial buildings with the intent to rent or sell them for a profit.

Unlike purchasing a primary residence, these properties aren't typically places where you'll live. However, property investments can still generate a steady income through renting out spaces. For example, you could buy a duplex or multifamily home and live in one unit while renting out the others. Similarly, you could purchase a commercial property for a business and lease part of it to tenants.

For many starting out in real estate, this type of investment may seem out of reach due to the capital requirements. However, in the next chapter, we'll discuss how pooling capital from multiple investors can make these opportunities more accessible even for beginners.

The bottom line: real estate as a path to wealth

Real estate has long been considered a solid and reliable investment option. Whether you're buying your first home or exploring the possibility of owning rental properties or REITs, real estate offers a tangible way to build equity and generate passive income over time. While there are barriers to entry, such as high upfront costs and ongoing maintenance, the potential rewards are substantial.

As we continue, remember that real estate is just one of the many investment vehicles you can consider as part of a diverse portfolio. Whether you're focused on personal homeownership or looking to invest in commercial properties, this asset class provides a range of opportunities to build wealth in both the short and long term.

3.5 Retirement Vehicles

In this section, we'll dive into retirement-specific investment vehicles such as 401(k) and 403(b) plans, individual retirement accounts (IRAs), Roth IRAs, and pension plans. These accounts are designed to help you save and invest for the future, ensuring you have a source of income during retirement.

Employer-sponsored retirement plans: 401(k)s and 403(b)s

Let's start with the two most common retirement vehicles: 401(k) and 403(b) plans. These plans are employer-sponsored, meaning they're set up by your employer to help you save for retirement. The key difference is that 403(b)s are typically available to employees of nonprofit organizations such as schools, hospitals, and religious institutions, whereas 401(k)s are used by for-profit businesses.

Both types of plans allow you to make pretax contributions, meaning that money is automatically deducted from your paycheck and invested into your retirement account. This money grows tax-deferred—you won't pay taxes on it until you withdraw the funds, typically at age fifty-nine and a half years or older.

One of the biggest advantages of 401(k)s and 403(b)s is the potential for employer contributions. Many employers will match your contributions up to a certain percentage (often 5 percent), which is essentially free money for your retirement savings. This means one of your first retirement goals should be to maximize the employer match—this is an easy way to boost your retirement savings. In the next chapter, we will discuss how to best take advantage of this opportunity.

There are a few important considerations to keep in mind with these plans. The investment options available to you are usually limited to a selection chosen by your employer, and early withdrawals from these plans come with penalties and taxes. Additionally, there are annual contribution limits for these accounts, which generally increase each year. Catch-up contributions are also available for those fifty and older, allowing you to save even more as you approach retirement.

Individual retirement accounts (IRAs)

Next, let's look at IRAs—a great way to supplement your 401(k) or 403(b). A traditional IRA also allows you to contribute pre-tax dollars, which means that the money you deposit reduces your taxable income for the year. This can be an effective strategy for saving on taxes today while your investments grow tax deferred. However, it is essential to be aware of the income limits that determine whether you can contribute to a traditional IRA.

If you want to explore an alternative, consider a Roth IRA. Unlike a traditional IRA, contributions to a Roth IRA are made with after-tax dollars. The advantage is that any growth in the account, as well as withdrawals in retirement, are typically tax-free. This can be particularly beneficial if you anticipate a higher tax bracket during retirement.

Both types of IRAs have the same contribution limits and catch-up options for those over fifty. The main difference lies in their tax treatment—traditional IRAs offer tax deductions upfront, while Roth IRAs provide tax-free withdrawals in retirement. It is always advisable to consult with a tax professional for personalized advice.

Pension plans: a different approach to retirement

Lastly, there are pension plans, or defined benefit plans, which are somewhat different from 401(k) s and IRAs. In these plans, the employer promises to pay you a fixed monthly benefit when you retire. This benefit is typically based on your years of service with the company and your salary during those years.

Unlike 401(k)s and IRAs, where you control the contributions and investments, pension plans are managed and funded by the employer (or sometimes a union). In most cases, the employer is responsible for financing the entire pension. While some plans require employee contributions, many offer them voluntarily.

The key advantage of pension plans is that the monthly payments you receive during retirement are predictable and often guaranteed. However, pension plans are usually more complex to establish and maintain, and they come with administration costs for employers. Despite this, pension plans are still quite common—according to recent reports, *over 70 percent of U.S. workers had access to employer-sponsored pensions, and 56 percent participated in them.*[37]

Conclusion: planning for your future

Retirement may feel far away, but it's crucial to start planning early. Whether it's through a 401(k), 403(b), IRA, Roth IRA, or pension plan, there are several vehicles available to help you build your retirement savings.

Each of these plans offers different tax advantages, contribution limits, and investment options, so it's essential to understand how each one works in relation to your own financial goals. In the next chapter, we'll discuss how to manage these accounts and adjust your contributions as you approach retirement. By starting early and making consistent contributions, you'll be better prepared for a comfortable retirement down the road.

Chapter Summary and Action Steps

This chapter explored various vehicles for wealth creation, categorizing them into five key types: equity-based, debt-based, cash and cash-equivalent, alternative investment, and retirement-specific vehicles.

Equity-based investments, such as stocks, ETFs, and mutual funds, offer high growth potential but carry market risk. Debt-based investments, primarily bonds, provide fixed-income returns with lower risk. Cash and cash-equivalent options, including savings accounts, CDs, and money market accounts, offer stability and liquidity but lower returns.

Alternative investments, particularly real estate, present opportunities for asset appreciation and rental income. Finally, retirement-specific vehicles like 401(k)s, IRAs, and pensions provide long-term savings benefits, often with tax advantages.

Each vehicle plays a role in a diversified investment strategy, balancing risk and reward to achieve long-term financial growth.

3. *Compile a list of your investment information*: Create a list of your investments and options. Create a spreadsheet or a *tab* in your existing spreadsheet from Action 1. Create four columns titled Date, Institution, Account Type, and Amount. Next, fill in the columns with information from your investment accounts. For example:
    - Savings, CDs, or Bonds
    - Employer 401(k), 403(b), or Pension

- Individual IRA or Roth IRA
- Rollover IRA

If you currently don't have any investments, research the options available. Check with your employer about any available plans or accounts. You may find that one is already set up for you. You can consult your manager or the human resources department for more information.

Chapter 4

Applying Wealth-Building Strategies

Wealth creation is a journey, not a one-size-fits-all formula.

In the previous chapters, we explored the fundamental concepts of building wealth, including the importance of mindset, financial discipline, and various investment vehicles that have historically contributed to financial success. By now, you may have started thinking about how these ideas apply to your own situation.

This chapter is where we bring everything together, moving beyond concepts and into actionable strategies tailored to different financial stages. Since every person's financial journey is unique, there's no single *right* way to build wealth. However, we can break down the process into clear, structured steps to help guide decision-making.

To make this chapter more approachable, we've divided it into three sections:

1. *Establishing a baseline*: Understanding where you stand financially and identifying key areas to improve.
2. *Retirement investment options*: Exploring different vehicles for long-term financial security.
3. *Beyond retirement*: Thinking ahead to wealth preservation, legacy planning, and financial independence.

By aligning financial decisions with personal goals, risk tolerance, and life circumstances, you can create a plan that works for you. Whether you are just starting out, working toward long-term stability, or thinking about financial independence, this chapter provides practical insights to help you make informed choices.

4.1 Establishing a Baseline

Before making any major financial decisions, it's essential to understand where you currently stand. Two key metrics can provide valuable insight into your financial health: net worth and credit rating.

- *Net worth* is the difference between what you own (assets) and what you owe (liabilities).
- *Credit* rating is a numerical representation of your creditworthiness, typically ranging from 300 to 850.

Knowing these two numbers gives you a starting point and helps shape your financial strategy. If you're new to wealth-building, don't be discouraged if your net worth is negative; many people begin at that point. What truly matters is having the knowledge to make improvements.

If you're starting from a place of debt, don't panic—I've been there too. The key is awareness and action.

Tracking your financial status

Fortunately, technology has made it easier than ever to monitor finances. Tools like Credit Karma can help you track your net worth and credit rating in real time. If you prefer a manual approach, you can calculate net worth by listing all assets (home value, car, savings, investments) and subtracting all liabilities (mortgage, loans, credit card debt).

You can obtain your credit report by contacting the consumer financial protection bureau or using free annual reports provided by credit bureaus. Reviewing your credit history regularly ensures accuracy and gives you the opportunity to dispute errors.

Understanding debt: the good and the bad

Debt can be a roadblock or a tool, depending on how it's managed.

- *Good debt* includes student loans and mortgages—investments that can increase future earnings or net worth.
- *Bad debt* includes high-interest credit cards and payday loans, which can quickly spiral into financial stress.

Addressing bad debt first is crucial to long-term financial stability. Strategies like the *debt snowball* (paying off small debts first) or *debt avalanche* (tackling high-interest debt first) can accelerate repayment.

If credit cards contribute to overspending, consider putting them away temporarily. Using cash for everyday expenses helps reinforce spending awareness and prevents unnecessary debt accumulation.

Building an emergency fund

Regardless of your debt status, an emergency fund is essential. Financial experts recommend saving *three to six months' worth of living expenses* to cover unexpected situations like job loss or medical emergencies.

To make saving easier, start small—automating transfers into a separate savings account can gradually build a strong financial safety net. High-yield savings accounts offer competitive interest rates, helping your emergency fund grow over time.

Improving your credit rating

A strong credit rating opens doors to better loan rates, housing opportunities, and financial flexibility. If your rating is low, focus on:

1. *Paying bills on time*: Even setting up autopay for minimum payments helps.
2. *Reducing credit card balances*
3. *Avoiding unnecessary credit applications*: Every hard inquiry affects your rating.

4. *Checking credit reports*: Review for errors and dispute inaccuracies.

Think of your credit history as a financial résumé—lenders want to see consistency and responsible credit management.

4.2 Retirement Investment Options

Once bad debt is under control and an emergency fund is established (or at least initiated), it's time to look toward the future. Retirement may seem far away, but starting early allows compound interest to work in your favor.

Employer-sponsored retirement plans (401(k) and **403(b))**

Typically, your employer-sponsored retirement plan is the best place to start. If you're not enrolled, ask your human resources department how. You'll want to begin investing in it as soon as possible, ideally contributing the maximum amount your employer will match—often 3–5 percent. Remember the money is pre-tax. Therefore, the more you invest in your employer-sponsored retirement plan, the less tax you pay. Several online calculators may help you understand the impact on your take-home pay, and your human resources department or your company's retirement brokerage can also assist.

Choosing funds and **understanding fees**

As you establish your employer-sponsored retirement account, you'll likely need to select which funds to invest in. Some companies automatically enroll employees in default options like "target date funds," which are structured around your expected retirement year (e.g., "the 2050 Fund"). While convenient, these funds often come with high fees that can erode investment returns over time.

Even a small percentage difference in fees can have a significant impact. While a small percentage or two might not seem significant, the costs can accumulate to tens of thousands, or even millions, of dollars over your investment career.

Figure 5 from the U.S. Securities and Exchange Commission illustrates that the difference between a 0.25 percent (*blue line*) and 1 percent (*green line*) annual fee over twenty years results in a $30,000 difference in the overall portfolio, based on an initial $100,000 investment.

Figure 5. Portfolio value from investing $100,000 over twenty years.[38]

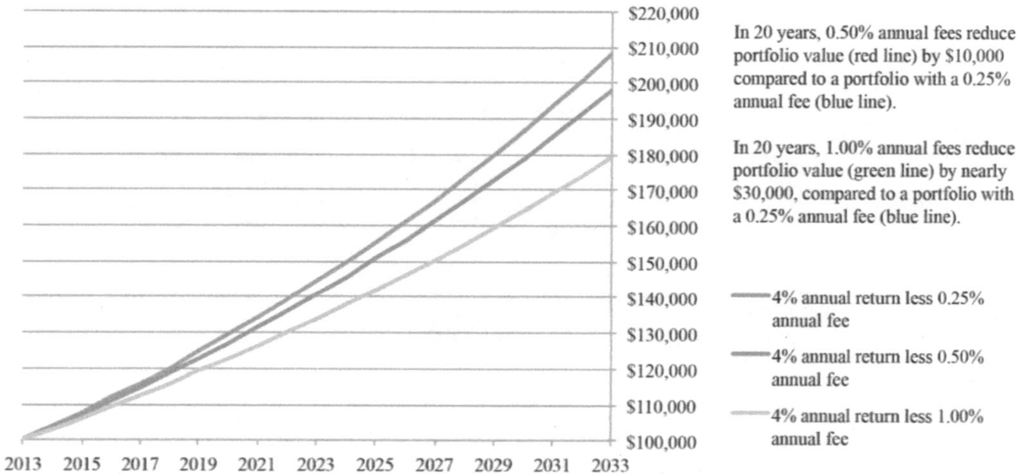

If the money was reinvested, as in Figure 6, not only would you have the initial investment (in the case of Figure 4, $28,000), but you would have also gained an additional $12,000 in interest.

Figure 6. Illustration of ongoing fees over twenty years.[39]

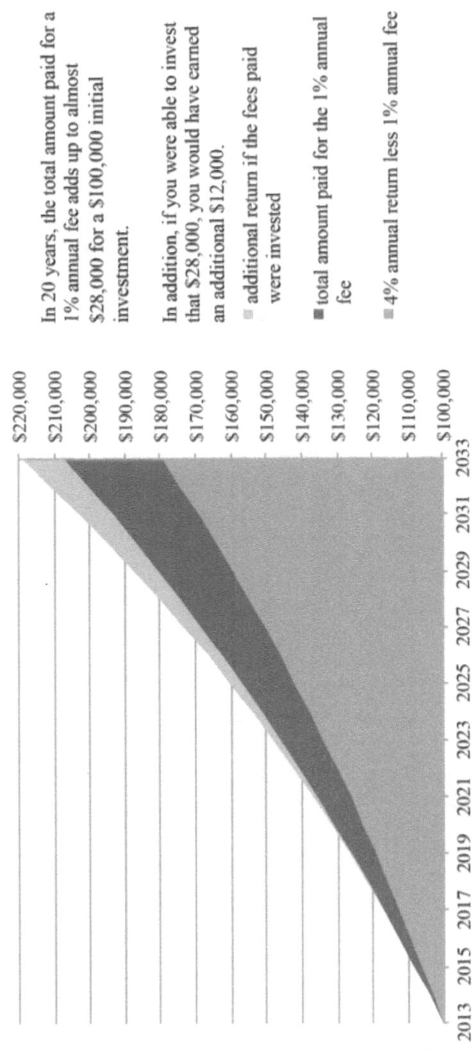

Additionally, most funds outside of index funds—such as actively managed funds—carry higher fees because they are managed by investors who attempt to *beat* the market. However, as Warrant argued, *low-cost index funds are a wise investment option for most people.*[40] In fact, Buffett famously bet *$1 million that an S&P 500 index fund could beat a selection of hand-picked hedge funds over ten years.*[41] The result was *Buffett comfortably won the wager.*[42]

As we reviewed in Chapter 3, index funds track a specific market index and involve little management, which results in lower fees—often as low as 0.02 percent. This makes them an excellent choice for passive investors.

Understanding your investment options

While you can choose which funds to invest in within your employer's retirement plan, your employer selects the brokerage (e.g., fidelity, empower financial) and determines which funds are available. Though this limits your options, the employer match and ease of investing usually outweigh these limitations.

Regardless, you will want to evaluate the available funds and select an appropriate asset allocation that suits your needs and position. Traditionally, this has been done based on age and risk level.

Asset allocation—how you distribute investments among stocks, bonds, and other assets—is crucial. Typically, younger investors can afford to take more risks, while those closer to retirement shift to a more conservative mix. Again, the reasoning is that the more years you have, the better you can endure market fluctuations and recover your earnings before needing them, and vice versa.

For example, an *aggressive* investor aged *twenty to thirty* might allocate:

- 95 percent stocks (large-cap index, mid-cap index, small-cap index, international index).
- 5 percent bonds (bond fund).

In contrast, as a conservative investor, the *twenty- to thirty-year-olds* might allocate:

- 80 percent stocks
- 20 percent bonds

As one reaches retirement age, that mix will likely shift to more bonds and possibly even cash investments (such as those discussed in Chapter 3) as the withdrawal age of fifty-nine and a half is reached.

Everyone will approach investing differently, whether you self-invest or have someone invest on your behalf. Just know that asset allocation guides are widely available from reputable brokerage firms to help you determine the right mix for your goals and risk tolerance (see Figure 7 from T. Rowe Price).

However, once you understand your asset allocation, you can explore the investment options available within your employer-sponsored account.

Figure 7. Retirement asset allocation models by age.[43]

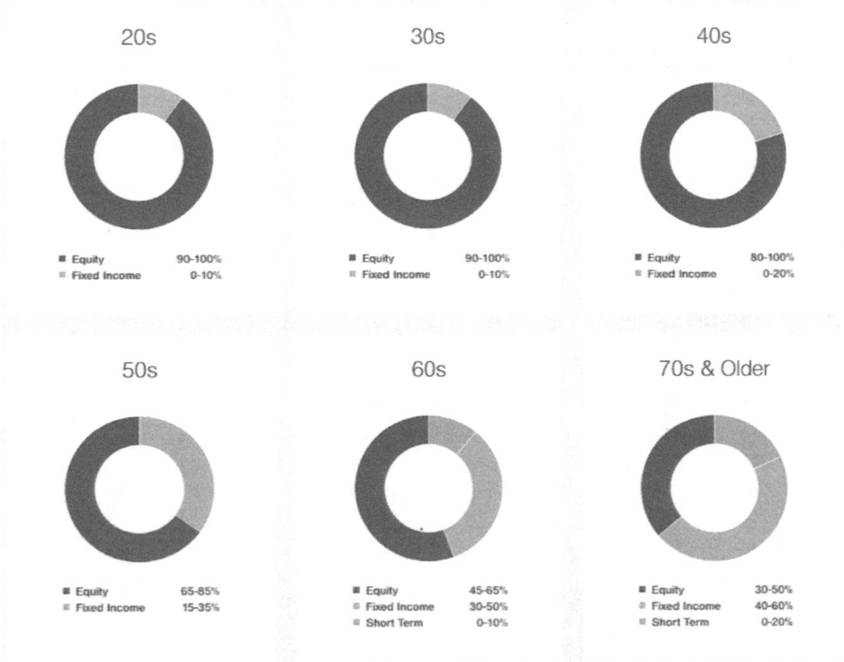

Managing your investments

Once your account is set up, you can access it through the brokerage's online portal to monitor your funds, track performance, and make adjustments. Employer-sponsored plans typically offer a limited number of funds—often ten to twenty—compared to the thousands available in the broader market. Nevertheless, you should familiarize yourself with the platform to research investments, buy/sell assets, and rebalance your portfolio. Whether you are investing through your employer's account or your own, this process remains the same.

Diversification is key to managing risk and maximizing returns. Within your employer-sponsored fund you will likely see options like:

- Large cap, mid cap, small cap, and international funds
- Index funds
- Bond funds
- Target date funds

The names of the funds usually provide clues about their types. For example, a "US Large-Cap Growth Index" fund is designed to invest in large-capitalization (value) US companies within an index; the specific index is sometimes included in the name but is mentioned in its strategy description.

Applying the aggressive asset allocation from the *twenty-to-thirty age* group mentioned earlier (*95 percent stocks*, 5 percent bonds), a well-diversified portfolio might allocate (totaling 100 percent of your investment):

- 25 percent large-cap index
- 25 percent mid-cap index
- 25 percent small-cap index
- 20 percent international index
- 5 percent bonds index

This mix spreads the risk and creates opportunities across various asset class types.

Staying in control of your investments

If the idea of managing investments feels overwhelming, don't worry; you're not alone. For most busy people (just about everyone), researching investments takes more time and energy than they can spare. The good news is you don't need to. We already mentioned one way to lighten the load: index funds. As Buffett remarked about investing in them, *you just have to sit back and let the American industry do its job for you.*[44]

If your employer's plan includes index funds, spreading your investments across different asset classes and adjusting your stock-bond-cash ratio as you near retirement is a solid strategy. If your plan doesn't offer index funds, use the brokerage's tools to compare fees (e.g., gross expense ratio) and Morningstar ratings to make informed decisions.

Maximizing contributions and rebalancing

Once your investments are set, aim to increase your contributions over time, up to the maximum allowed by the IRS. As of this writing, the annual limit is $23,500 annually, with an additional $7,500 *catch-up* contribution allowed for individuals aged fifty and older.

It's important to review your portfolio at least once a year to rebalance it. Rebalancing means buying or selling assets to return the portfolio to its intended allocation. This process helps ensure that your desired asset allocation aligns with your financial goals.

Two key reasons to rebalance are:

1. *Maintain risk tolerance*: Rebalancing helps keep the portfolio within your preferred level of risk (see section 4.2).

2. *Optimizing returns*: It allows you to capture gains and effectively manage downside risk.

For example, if one of your funds outperforms and your portfolio shifts from 95 percent stocks and 5 percent bonds to 90 percent stocks and 10 percent bonds, you must rebalance your investments to reflect your strategy accurately.

Even if your strategy and timeline stay the same, you might notice that certain funds have outperformed others. Using our earlier 25/25/25/20/5 plan, your international index fund may now represent 30 percent of your overall portfolio after outperforming the others. Rebalancing will redistribute funds to help you maintain your targeted allocation of 25/25/25/20/5.

The importance of rebalancing lies in minimizing risk by ensuring that riskier asset classes, such as stocks, do not increasingly dominate your portfolio. It's essential to remember that you can sell and transfer money within the portfolio without incurring any penalties. Early withdrawal penalties only apply when funds are taken out of the account.

Additionally, some brokerages allow for automatic rebalancing, allowing you to set a scheduled (often annually) rebalance to maintain your desired mix. However, I caution relying solely on this feature, as it can be easy to forget. Over time, your needs may change, especially as you approach retirement, so it's wise to adjust your strategy accordingly. Setting a yearly calendar reminder to review your portfolio is a good habit to develop.

What happens when you change jobs?

If you separate from your employer, you have several options with your retirement account:

1. Leave the funds in your employer's plan (if allowed).
2. Roll them over to your new employer's plan (if available).
3. Transfer them to a rollover IRA (recommended for flexibility and more investment choices).
4. Cash out (not recommended due to significant early withdrawal penalties and taxes).

A rollover IRA is often the best choice because it consolidates retirement savings into one account, making it easier to manage. With frequent job changes becoming the norm, tracking multiple 401(k) accounts can be challenging. Although it may seem surprising, as of *May 2023, 29.2 million 401k accounts had been forgotten*—amounting to roughly *25 percent of all 401k assets in the U.S.*[45]

A rollover IRA also provides access to a broader range of investment options, allowing for better portfolio customization.

If you decide to keep your money in your previous employer's account, be sure to check for any withdrawal restrictions if you choose to move later. Sometimes, there is a timeframe—such as ninety days from the date of separation—during which you must complete a rollover, or the money will remain in the account.

Final thoughts

Investing for retirement can seem daunting at first, but with the right approach, it becomes much more manageable. Start early, take advantage of employer matching contributions, keep fees low, and diversify your investments. By making informed choices now, you'll set yourself up for financial security in the future.

4.3 Beyond Retirement

Once you've maximized your employer-sponsored retirement accounts, you have several options to continue building wealth. One of the most popular is a Roth IRA, which allows you to contribute *after-tax dollars* that grow *tax-free*. Unlike traditional retirement accounts, which are tax-deferred and incur taxes upon withdrawal, Roth IRAs are tax-free and are also exempt from taxes at withdrawal. Since tax rates tend to rise over time, balancing traditional and Roth accounts helps maximize your future income.

Another key advantage of a Roth IRA is flexibility—you can withdraw your original contributions anytime without taxes or penalties. However, earnings on those contributions may be subject to restrictions, so it's essential to understand the rules. As with other retirement accounts, the IRS contribution limits apply. At the time of this writing, the annual limit is $7,000 (or $8,000 if you're over age fifty), so be sure to check the latest guidelines and consult your tax professional.

Alternative wealth-building options

Beyond retirement accounts, diversifying your investments can help manage risk and create additional income streams. Depending on your risk tolerance, you might consider:

- *High-yield savings accounts* and *money market accounts*: Ideal for short-term savings

goals, such as a home down payment or emergency fund, while still earning interest.
- *Certificates of deposit* (CDs): A low-risk option that locks in a fixed interest rate over a set period.

As noted earlier, these alternative options, including high-yield savings accounts, are excellent for accumulating wealth when preparing for a specific need, such as a down payment on a home or a new car.

Real estate as an investment

Real estate can be a powerful tool for wealth-building and portfolio diversification, but entering the market—especially after purchasing your first home—can be challenging. One way to reduce financial barriers is by pooling resources with friends, family, or trusted investors. By partnering with others, you can lower individual risk and capital requirements, making real estate more accessible. However, it's critical to align on objectives and document agreements in writing—seeking legal guidance is highly recommended.

If you have home improvement skills, you can further reduce costs by handling the renovations yourself. Many buyers prefer move-in ready homes, which creates opportunities to purchase undervalued properties, make improvements, and either sell for a profit or rent for ongoing income. If real estate becomes a passion, obtaining a real estate license could further reduce costs and open up more opportunities.

Chapter Summary and Action Steps

This chapter brought together the earlier wealth creation concepts and focuses on applying them through practical strategies. Wealth-building is unique to everyone, but it can be structured into three main sections: establishing a financial baseline, retirement investment options, and planning beyond retirement.

The chapter begins by emphasizing the importance of understanding net worth and credit rating as foundational financial metrics. Net worth is the difference between total assets and liabilities, while a credit rating reflects financial responsibility. Tools like Credit Karma can assist in tracking these metrics, but manual calculations are also an option. Managing debt, particularly differentiating between *good debt* (e.g., student loans, mortgages) and *bad debt* (e.g., high-interest credit cards), is crucial for financial stability. Strategies for paying off debt include increasing income, leveraging home equity, or utilizing employer-sponsored 401(k) loans. Additionally, building an emergency fund with three to six months' worth of expenses also provides a financial safety net.

Once bad debt is addressed, retirement investment becomes the next focus. Employer-sponsored retirement plans, such as 401(k)s, should be prioritized, particularly maximizing employer matching contributions. The chapter advises against high-fee "target date funds" in favor of low-cost index funds, citing Warren Buffett's advocacy for them as a reliable long-term strategy for most investors. Asset allocation—dividing investments across different categories like large-cap, medium-cap, and small-cap stocks, as well as bonds—is essential for balancing risks and returns. Rebalancing investments periodically ensures that the portfolio remains aligned with the financial goals.

Finally, the chapter highlights the importance of continuous financial education and making informed wealth-building decisions. Whether managing investments independently or seeking professional guidance, understanding financial principles puts individuals in control of their financial future.

4. *Establish your baseline:*
    - Download Credit Karma and link your accounts. Make note of and review your credit rating and net worth. Review your credit rating summary to understand factors that influence your rating, and check your report for any errors—if you find any, be sure to dispute them.
    - Review your debts and identify any outstanding credit cards or other bad debts that need your attention.
    - Have you opened a high-yield or money market account to start building your emergency fund?

5. *Retirement investment:*
    - Are you contributing to your employer-sponsored retirement or pension?
    - Have you maximized the employer's matching contributions?
    - Can you increase your contributions?
    - Log into the plan's account. What funds are you invested in? Are there better funds with lower fees? Is the asset mix aligned with your goals? When was the last time it was rebalanced?

- Do you have a reminder on your calendar to rebalance again next year?
- Do you have investments in other employers' accounts that should be moved to your current employer or its own rollover account?

6. *Beyond retirement*: If your employer retirement account is at the max contribution limit, it may be time to look at other investment options.
    - Do you have after-tax money you could invest in a Roth IRA?
    - Are you interested in owning real estate? Consider your situation: would you prefer to buy and hold property such as land? Pool finances with friends, family, or colleagues? Invest in rental properties? Or are you hoping to flip homes after making improvements?

Conclusion

In conclusion, *A Beginner's Guide to Wealth Creation* explores the current investment landscape in the United States. It reinforced the importance of taking control of your finances rather than letting them control you. It emphasized the need to shift your money mindset, align investment priorities with personal needs, and recognize the advantages of investing early.

Additionally, it underscored the importance of earning more than you spend, reducing debt, and increasing investments. It explored five primary vehicles for wealth creation, clarified several industry terms, and structured the approach into three sections to provide clear roadmaps for success.

I sincerely hope you found this information helpful and inspired you to continue learning—using this knowledge as a springboard toward greater financial security. Remember, this is just the beginning, and every step brings you closer to your goals, no matter how small. I wish you success on your financial journey!

Appendix

Activity Checklist

1. *Start tracking your spending:* Create a spreadsheet with four columns—date, debit, credit, and category. In the debit column, list all money spent, including expenses from credit cards and bank statements. In the credit column, record any money earned. For each transaction, provide a brief description in the category column, such as *dining out*, *vehicle expense*, and so on, but keep them consistent (for example, under vehicle expenses, include gas, repairs, and accessories such as air fresheners).
   - Be sure to include the date of each transaction. Work backward for three months,

then total up both the debit and credit columns. Is there more money in the debit than credit? Which categories are you spending the most? Are there areas where you can save?

- Note: While it may be tempting to use automated processes to track your spending, it's important to do this manually, especially at the beginning. This will help you gain a clearer understanding of where your money is going (even if you think you do).

2. *Access your money mindset:* Create a three-to-five-year plan. Be realistic, but the goals you create should challenge you. Start by considering the following:
    - *Personal development:* What skills, certifications, or degrees do you want to acquire? Are there specific areas you want to focus on, such as health, relationships, or personal growth?
    - *Career:* Where do you want to be in your career? Are you looking for a promotion, a career change, or a new skill set?
    - *Finances:* Does your employer offer education assistance? Are there any spending

habits identified in step one that need to change? Begin identifying your debt (we will discuss more in Chapter 4).

- *Break down long-term plans into actionable goals*: What do you need to do this year, this month, and today to achieve these goals?

3. *Compile a list of your investment information:* Create a list of your investments and options. Create a spreadsheet or a "tab" in your existing spreadsheet from Action 1. Create four columns titled date, institution, account type, and amount. Next, fill in the columns with information from your investment accounts. For example:
    - Savings, CDs, or Bonds
    - Employer 401(k), 403(b), or pension
    - Individual IRA or Roth IRA
    - Rollover IRA

If you currently don't have any investments, research the investment options available to you. Check with your employer about any available plans or accounts. You may find that one is already set up for you. You can consult your manager or the human resources department for more information.

4. *Establish your baseline:*
    - Download Credit Karma and link your accounts. Make note of and review your credit rating and net worth. Review your credit rating summary to understand factors that influence your rating, and check your report for any errors—if you find any, be sure to dispute them.
    - Review your debts and identify any outstanding credit cards or other bad debts that need your attention.
    - Have you opened a high-yield or money market account to start building your emergency fund?

5. *Retirement investment:*
    - Are you contributing to your employer-sponsored retirement or pension?
    - Are you maximizing the employer's matching contributions?
    - Can you increase your contributions?
    - Log into the plan's account. What funds are you invested in? Are there better funds with lower fees? Is the asset mix aligned with your goals? When was the last time it was rebalanced?

- Do you have a reminder on your calendar to rebalance again next year?
- Do you have investments in other employers' accounts that should be moved to your current employer or its own rollover account?

6. *Beyond retirement:* If your employer retirement account is at the max contribution limit, it may be time to look at other investment options.
    - Do you have after-tax money you could invest in a Roth IRA?
    - Are you interested in owning real estate? Consider your situation: would you prefer to buy and hold property such as land? Pool finances with friends, family, or colleagues? Invest in rental properties? Or are you hoping to flip homes after making improvements?

Glossary of Financial Terms

actively managed funds: Funds use their research and judgement to buy and sell securities to attempt to beat the market.

aggressive investor: High-risk, high-reward approach to investing.

APY (annual percentage yield): The effective rate of return on an investment for one year taking compounding interest into account.

asset allocation: Dividing your investments among different assets such as stocks, bonds, and cash.

average annual return: Average yearly return on an investment calculated by dividing the total return by the number of years.

bad debt: Debt you are likely unable to repay, such as high-interest credit cards.

bond: A fixed-income investment that represents a loan made by an investor to a borrower, usually corporate or government.

bond duration: A measurement of how much a bond's price will change in response to interest rate changes.

bond funds: A collection of bonds that are pooled together and sold to investors as shares, such as a mutual or exchange-traded fund.

broker: A person or company that buys and sells securities on behalf of an investor.

company match: When an employer contributes money to an employee's retirement account based on how much the employee contributes.

compound interest: Interest that you earn on interest. Accumulated from a principal sum and previously accumulated interest.

conservative investor: Someone who avoids risk in return for a steady income and capital preservation.

coupons: Interest paid to a bondholder on a set schedule until the bond matures.

credit rating: An estimate of persons or organizations ability to fulfill their financial commitments based on previous dealings, typically represented by a rating ranging from 300 to 850.

delayed gratification: Ability to resist immediate reward in favor of a more valuable reward later.

discount brokerage: A company that buys and sells investments for clients at a lower fee.

diversification: A financial strategy that involves spreading investments across different asset classes, industries, or regions to reduce risk while attempting to maximize returns.

Dow Jones Industrial Average (The DOW): A stock market index that tracks thirty large, publicly owned companies trading on the New York Stock Exchange.

economic trends: The general direction of an economy over time.

emergency fund: Money saved for unexpected expenses such as home repairs, car repairs of job loss.

employer sponsored plan(s): A benefit that an employer offers to their employees (education, retirement, etc.).

equity based: The ownership interest in a company's assets.

FDIC (Federal Deposit Insurance Company): A government agency that insures deposits in banks and savings associations.

financial independence: Having sufficient money to cover living expenses without relying on employment or others. It also encompasses the freedom to make choices that align with your values and goals.

financial literacy: Ability to manage money wisely and make informed financial decisions.

fixed-income securities: Debt instruments that pay a fixed interest rate over a set period of time (e.g., bonds).

full-service brokerage: A licensed financial firm that offers a wide variety of services to clients including research and advice, retirement planning, and tax tips.

good debt: Money borrowed to achieve a financial goal, like buying a home or obtaining an education.

index: Measures the performance of a basket of securities (e.g., Dow or S&P 500).

index funds: A mutual or exchange-traded fund (ETF) that mirrors an index's performance by investing in the same funds that make up the index.

international funds: A mutual fund that invests in companies outside of an investor's home country.

investing: Allocating funds today to generate more wealth in the future.

investment strategy: Principles guiding an investor's decisions based on goals, risk tolerance and future capital needs.

IRA (individual retirement account): A tax-advantaged investment account that assists you in saving for retirement.

laborer: A person who works in manual labor.

large cap: Denoting or relating to the stock of a company with a large capitalization (typically more than $10 billion).

leader: Someone to look up to—a person who guides, helps, listens, and teaches.

maturity date: The date on which the principal amount of a note is due (e.g., bond).

mid-cap: Denoting or relating to the stock of a company with a medium capitalization (typically $2 to $10 billion).

Nasdaq: National Association of Securities Dealers Automated Quotations: A stock exchange based in New York City.

net worth: The value of all assets minus the value of all liabilities.

NYSE: New York Stock Exchange: A stock exchange based in New York City.

passively managed funds: An investment vehicle that aims to replicate the performance of a specific market index, such as the S&P 500, by maintaining the same proportion of holdings as the index.

pension plan: An employee benefit program created by an employer or by an employee organization, such as a union, that provides retirement income or defers income until termination of covered employment or beyond.

portfolio: A selection of investments, such as stocks, bonds, and real estate, that are owned by an investor or institution.

Roth IRA: A tax-advantaged retirement account where you contribute money after taxes have been deducted.

S&P 500: Standard and Poor's 500 is an index which tracks roughly five hundred publicly traded companies based in the United States.

securities: Are negotiable financial instruments that have a financial value, typically in the form of stocks, bonds, or options.

small-cap: Denoting or relating to the stock of a company with a small capitalization (typically $250 million to $10 billion).

strategic planning: Creating a long-term roadmap to achieve financial objectives by analyzing your current financial situation, setting specific objectives, and developing strategies and tactics to reach them.

target date funds: A type of investment that automatically adjusts its asset allocation as the target date approaches.

wealth-building: Process of increasing your financial assets over time by earning, saving, and investing.

References

1 K. McNair, "18 states require personal finance education in schools-here's what they're teaching kids about money," Accessed: Jan. 30, 2025, [Online], Available: https://www.cnbc.com/2023/04/13/how-personal-finance-is-taught-in-us-schools.html.

2 Federal Reserve, "Retirement and Investments," Accessed: Jan. 06, 2025. [Online], Available: https://www.federalreserve.gov/publications/2023-economic-well-being-of-us-households-in-2022-retirement-investments.html.

3 P. Fore, "Why is Gen Z suddenly flocking to this college course that's been taught for decades," Yahoo Finance. Accessed: Feb. 18, 2025. [Online]. Available: https://finance.yahoo.com/news/why-gen-z-suddenly-flocking-080100585.html.

4 D. de Visé, "Living paycheck to paycheck is more common than you think, and it isn't always bad," USA TODAY. Accessed: Feb. 18, 2025. [Online]. Available: https://www.usatoday.com/story/money/2024/12/05/living-paycheck-to-paycheck-debt/76733415007/.

5 Federal Reserve, "Retirement and Investments." Accessed: Jan. 06, 2025. [Online]. Available: https://www.federalreserve.gov/

publications/2023-economic-well-being-of-us-households-in-2022-retirement-investments.html.

6 Federal Reserve, "Retirement and Investments."

7 Federal Reserve, "Retirement and Investments."

8 Federal Reserve, "Retirement and Investments."

9 Federal Reserve, "Retirement and Investments."

10 W. Hopler, "Famous Quotes on Financial Stability and Well-Being," Center for the Advancement of Well-Being. Accessed: Dec. 12, 2024. [Online]. Available: https://wellbeing.gmu.edu/famous-quotes-on-financial-stability-and-well-being/

11 S. DiSalvo, "5 Huge Lies About Generational Wealth," Yahoo Finance. Accessed: Dec. 12, 2024. [Online]. Available: https://finance.yahoo.com/news/5-huge-lies-generational-wealth-181719865.html.

12 *Cambridge Dictionary, bias.* Accessed: Jan. 13, 2025. [Online]. Available: https://dictionary.cambridge.org/us/dictionary/english/bias.

13 R. M. Doroghazi, "'Quotes from Warren Buffett: Part I of II,'" *Am. J. Cardiol.*, vol. 163, pp. 132–133, Jan. 2022, doi: 10.1016/j.amjcard.2021.10.009.

14 S. Eckhart and B. Glasner, "Who's left out of America's retirement savings system?," Economic Innovation Group. Accessed: Jan. 22, 2025. [Online]. Available: https://eig.org/whos-left-out-of-americas-retirement-savings-system/

15 NASAA, "Compound Interest," NASAA. Accessed: Dec. 18, 2024. [Online]. Available: https://www.nasaa.org/investor-education/millennial-money-mission/compound-interest-2/.

16 Ibid.

17 M. Leonhardt, "If you're afraid to invest in the stock market, do this calculation to see how much money you're losing out

on," CNBC. Accessed: Jan. 07, 2025. [Online]. Available: https://www.cnbc.com/2019/10/25/if-youre-afraid-of-the-market-calculate-how-much-money-youre-losing.html.

18 Ibid.

19 Ibid.

20 Gallup, "What Percentage of Americans Own Stock?" Gallup.com. Accessed: Dec. 18, 2024. [Online]. Available: https://news.gallup.com/poll/266807/percentage-americans-owns-stock.aspx.

21 Ibid.

22 Ibid.

23 Ibid.

24 S. McLeod, "Maslow's Hierarchy of Needs." Accessed: Dec. 18, 2024. [Online]. Available: https://www.simplypsychology.org/maslow.html.

25 Ibid.

26 J. M. Lee and S. D. Hanna, "Savings Goals and Saving Behavior From a Perspective of Maslow's Hierarchy of Needs," *J. Financ. Couns. Plan.*, vol. 26, no. 2, pp. 129–147, Nov. 2015, doi: 10.1891/1052-3073.26.2.129.

27 B. Pokora and J. Moralas, "Average Credit Card Debt Study 2025," Forbes Advisor. Accessed: Jan. 22, 2025. [Online]. Available: https://www.forbes.com/advisor/credit-cards/average-credit-card-debt/.

28 Ibid.

29 R. M. Doroghazi, "'Quotes from Warren Buffett: Part II of II,'" *Am. J. Cardiol.*, vol. 164, pp. 131–132, Feb. 2022, doi: 10.1016/j.amjcard.2021.10.031.

30 P. A. Diamond, "What stock market returns to expect for the future?," *Soc Sec Bull*, vol. 63, no. 2, p. 38, 2000.

[31] Library of Congress, "Research Guides: Wall Street and the Stock Exchanges: Historical Resources: Stock Exchanges," Library of Congress. Accessed: Dec. 30, 2024. [Online]. Available: https://guides.loc.gov/wall-street-history/exchanges

[32] P. A. Diamond, "What Stock Market Returns to Expect for the Future?" *Soc. Secur. Bull.*, vol. 63, no. 2, 2000.

[33] R. M. Doroghazi, "'Quotes from Warren Buffett: Part I of II,'" *Am. J. Cardiol.*, vol. 163, pp. 132–133, Jan. 2022, doi: 10.1016/j.amjcard.2021.10.009.

[34] S&P Global, "About Us," About Us. Accessed: Jan. 01, 2025. [Online]. Available: https://www.spglobal.com/spdji/en/about-us/

[35] Fidelity, "The bond market | When issuers declare bankruptcy | Fidelity." Accessed: Dec. 31, 2024. [Online]. Available: https://www.fidelity.com/learning-center/investment-products/fixed-income-bonds/when-bonds-go-bad.

[36] Federal Reserve Economic Data, "Average Sales Price of Houses Sold for the United States," Federal Reserve Economic Data. Accessed: Jan. 02, 2025. [Online]. Available: https://fred.stlouisfed.org/graph/?g=CpFW.

[37] J. J. Topoleski, E. A. Myers, and S. L. Bryan, "Worker Participation in Employer-Sponsored Pensions: Data in Brief and Recent Trends," *Congr. Res. Serv.*, vol. R43439, Sep. 2024, [Online]. Available: https://crsreports.congress.gov/product/pdf/R/R43439.

[38] SEC, "Investor Bulletin: How Fees and Expenses Affect Your Investment Portfolio," vol. 164.

[39] Ibid.

[40] A. Volenik, "Warren Buffett Bet $1M He Could Outperform Hedge Funds Over A Decade. He Did It With A Strategy Requiring No Investing Skill," Yahoo Finance. Accessed: Jan.

16, 2025. [Online]. Available: https://finance.yahoo.com/news/warren-buffett-bet-1m-could-151520090.html

41 Ibid.

42 Ibid.

43 T. RowePrice, "T. Rowe Price Personal Investor - Asset Allocation Models and Planning." Accessed: Feb. 21, 2025. [Online]. Available: https://www.troweprice.com/personal-investing/resources/planning/asset-allocation-planning.html.

44 A. Volenik, "Warren Buffett Bet $1M He Could Outperform Hedge Funds Over A Decade. He Did It With A Strategy Requiring No Investing Skill," Yahoo Finance.

45 C. Beiber, "Americans forgot about $1.65 trillion in retirement savings — here's how to find and reclaim your lost money," Yahoo Finance. Accessed: Jan. 23, 2025. [Online]. Available: https://finance.yahoo.com/news/americans-forgot-1-65-trillion-143300193.html

About the Author

Brett Pichla, a Detroit native, has over twenty-five years of corporate experience, spanning small businesses to Fortune 250 companies. With bachelor's and master's degrees in business administration specializing in leadership, he is pursuing a doctorate in business administration at Florida International University. Brett is passionate about continuous learning and business success and balances his career with a vibrant personal life. Married for over twenty years, he enjoys traveling, backpacking, scuba diving, cycling, playing guitar, fitness, movies, and reading. His commitment to growth and achievement defines his professional journey and personal pursuits.

www.ingramcontent.com/pod-product-compliance
Lightning Source LLC
LaVergne TN
LVHW090419210926
848480LV00002B/625
9798896176213